Carving Clowns & Circus Wagons

Carving Clowns & Circus Wagons

Billy J. Smith

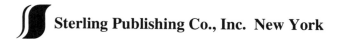 Sterling Publishing Co., Inc. New York

Dedicated to my grandchildren. May this book help to in-
spire them to become involved in a satisfying hobby and
their mates to be as tolerant and understanding about it as
their grandmother has been about mine.

Library of Congress Cataloging-in-Publication Data

Smith, Billy J.
    Carving clowns & circus wagons / by Billy J. Smith.
      p.   cm.
    Includes index.
    ISBN 0-8069-8744-8
    1. Wood-carving.   2. Clowns in art.
    3. Circus wagons in art.   I. Title.
  II. Title: Carving clowns and circus wagons.
    TT199.7.S65   1993
    731.4'62—dc20   92-35289
                                           CIP

10 9 8 7 6 5 4 3 2 1

Published in 1993 by Sterling Publishing Company, Inc.
387 Park Avenue South, New York, N.Y. 10016
© 1993 by Billy J. Smith
Distributed in Canada by Sterling Publishing
℅ Canadian Manda Group, P.O. Box 920, Station U
Toronto, Ontario, Canada M8Z 5P9
Distributed in Great Britain and Europe by Cassell PLC
Villiers House, 41/47 Strand, London WC2N 5JE, England
Distributed in Australia by Capricorn Link Ltd.
P.O. Box 665, Lane Cove, NSW 2066
Manufactured in the United States of America
All rights reserved

Sterling ISBN 0-8069-8744-8

Acknowledgments

To Charles Nurnberg of Sterling Publishing Co., Inc., for gently prodding and encouraging me to write another book.

To Jim Roberts for the inspiration I received from his book, *Clown Makeup*.

To Landmark Calendars for the great clown photos on their 1990 calendar.

To my family, friends, and neighbors for their comments and encouragement as they watched the building progress on the clowns and bandwagon pictured in this book.

Contents

Color section follows page 64

Preface

The Greatest Show on Earth! When Barnum and Bailey made this statement in giant bright-colored posters, they had no fear of contradiction. From the youngest to the oldest person in the crowd the thrill of the circus is never forgotten. From the side show to the bears, elephants, lions, tigers, aerial artists, popcorn, and candy, everything is exciting and memorable. But when the final act is over and the workers have packed and loaded all the equipment and animals and headed for the next show, the most vivid memories will be of the clowns, the music, and the parade. Regardless of age, color, or status, everyone loves a clown, a parade, and the exciting music of a circus band.

More than 500,000 people from all over the world each year thrill to Milwaukee's Great Circus Parade held in early July. Seventy-five priceless antique circus wagons are hauled from their home in the Circus Museum in Baraboo, Wisconsin, by a half-mile-long train. Twenty-five hundred volunteers, 750 horses, scores of wild animals, clowns, bands, and circus performers travel the 4½-mile route past throngs of excited onlookers from every walk of life.

My wife and I watched this giant spectacle in 1991 and we both agreed that the real stars of the show were the more than 100 clowns, the sound of the bands, and the beauty of the giant horses. Despite the magnificence of all the rest, if one took away the clowns, the bands, and the horses, there wouldn't be any circus parade.

I knew, before the parade had barely started, that I had to make my own circus parade. I had already made a display of several animated clowns to attract attention at a woodcarving show. I had already written a book, *Carving Horses and Carriages with Power Tools*, published by Sterling Publishing Co., Inc., New York. I knew how to make the horses, harnesses, wagons, and clowns. All I had to do was to design a circus bandwagon, search for miniature band instruments, and refine my clown patterns, and I could have my very own miniature circus parade.

Several neighbors stopped daily to watch the progress as my bandwagon and band were being built. They seemed to be nearly as excited by it as I was—more proof that everybody loves a parade, bands, and clowns!

There are millions of woodworkers, craftspeople, carvers, and painters, all with varying levels of skills. The accomplished "purist" woodcarver insists that a carving must be done using a sharp knife and then left unfinished to show the wood grain. He can reproduce the most minute details—facial expressions, veins, and eyeballs with the simple cut of a knife. Some of these accomplished carvers dismiss anyone who uses paints, power tools, or other methods to produce the same product.

If an artist can produce a work that's colorful, interesting, and properly proportioned, attracting attention and favorable comments, he will be rewarded with the satisfaction of a job well done. If his work is well done and enjoyable, people won't ask (and won't care) if he made every part with a sharp knife or if he purchased some of the parts at a craft shop. They like the overall appearance and they'll be amazed that he could blend a group of almost unrelated parts to form a piece of art.

I recognize that different people have different levels of skills. I wrote this book to offer suggestions and options on how to make realistic clowns regardless of the reader's skills. I describe which parts I have used purchased from craft shops, how to make the unavailable parts, how to paint them, what tools I use, and I suggest different methods to display the clowns, including plans for the bandwagon. The reader will find several methods for making the heads (the most complicated parts for most people), carved, or sculpted, from materials such as craft-shop wood or Styrofoam.®

My goal in this book is to show the "average" craftsperson how to produce clowns, and how to display them in an attractive setting. The reader can doubtless improve on some of my methods and suggestions. The reader may do the woodwork and ask someone else to do the painting. There's nothing wrong with that. When the project is completed, family and friends won't ask *how* you did it, they'll just marvel at the fact that you actually made it!

My satisfaction comes from knowing that I've helped someone to share the enjoyment I get from doing craft work. One of my greatest thrills was seeing a fire engine and hose cart in a big carving show in Davenport, Iowa, and knowing that they were made from plans in my first book by a man whom I had never known or met. I'd love to see the readers' finished projects and to hear their questions and remarks. The publishers of this book will forward your letters. Have fun, and relive the thrill of the circus parade!

1
Tools

You'll need a minimum number of shop tools to make the projects described in this book. You'll need basic shop tools like a radial arm saw or a table saw, a belt sander, and a disc sander (or use a small 1″ belt-and-disc combination). You'll also need a band saw or a scroll saw, and a drill press. You'll need sandpaper and whatever equipment you use to sand other projects. Small battery-operated drills like the ones shown in Illus. 1-1 are very handy, and you probably have at least one in your shop. I use a Dremel moto-tool and a Dremel drill press stand, as shown in Illus. 1-2.

A tool that can be found in most well-equipped shops is a Dremel-type moto-tool with a flex cable. There are several very good brands of power-tool carvers, such as Foredom, Pfingst, Master Carver, Sears (made by Dremel), and all

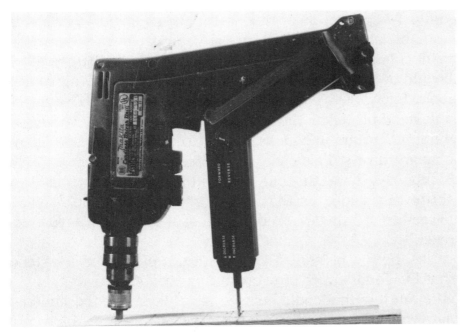

Illus. 1-1. *Two sizes of portable battery-operated drills. There are many fine brands of these available.*

Illus. 1-2. *A Dremel moto-tool and drill press*

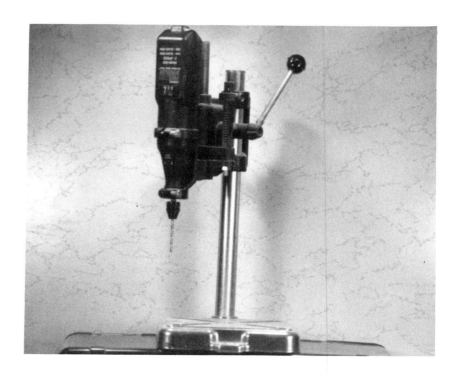

work very well. You can also use a common flex cable that attaches to an electric drill or motor, or even to your radial arm saw. I first started power-tool carving with a Dremel a few years ago because I didn't know how to carve with a knife. The power tool looked faster and simpler to me. It was available at my local hardware store, it came with an assortment of basic cutters, and it was on sale! Since then, I've bought every cutter I've found and I've added several moto-tools. I now use a bank of five tools, so that with the replaceable hand pieces on the two larger motors, I can have seven different cutters in chucks, ready to cut without stopping to change cutters. I also use a drill press and a router.

Illus. 1-3 shows this bank of five tools with a short description of each. For the projects shown in this book, the lowest-priced single-speed moto-tool (#275) is all you'd ever need.

The top row of Illus. 1-4 shows three cutters and one stone that I used for entire projects in this book. There are many other cutters that could be used, and I've shown these alternative cutters in the bottom row of the same photo. I haven't

Illus. 1-3. *My bank of moto-tools. Right to left: (1) My original power tool after over 6 years of hard use; (2) #275 single speed; (3) #395 variable speed; (4) Pfingst unit handles up to ¼″ shank cutters; (5) Dremel's #732, a ⅕ h.p. unit that takes up to ¼″ shank cutters. Units that are powerful enough to handle the ¼″ shanks are great for fast wood removal with the carbide Kutzall-type cutters; the hand pieces are easily switched to the smaller sizes for more detailed carving. If you're buying your first unit or upgrading, you'll never be sorry for buying the bigger tools. The #275 single-speed will do everything you need done for the projects in this book.*

shown any sanding or finishing equipment, because every woodworker has his own sanding methods and equipment. I use a rubber-backed drum sander with a ¼″ shank. This sander is fast, but it won't reach the detailed areas on the clowns. I use a homemade bow-type sander with 1″-wide emery cloth and regular sandpaper to reach these areas. The cutters pictured here are available in most good hardware and hobby shops. There are many other brands and types available in carving catalogs and shops.

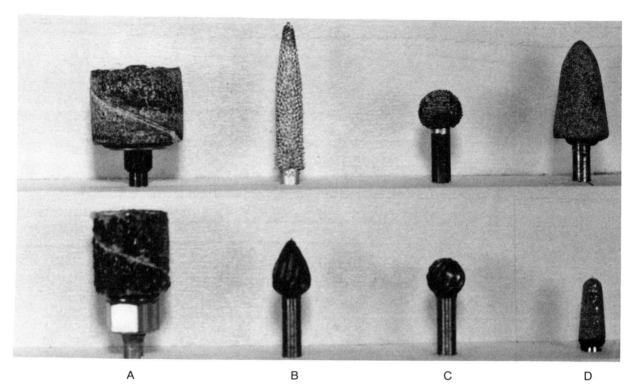

A   B   C   D

Illus. 1-4. *The cutters in the top row are the ones used for the projects shown in this book. The bottom row contains cutters that could be used. Dremel model numbers are used for convenience. A. #407 ½" drum sander. Fine, medium, and coarse bands are available. An optional ⅜" drum sander may get into tight areas. B. #9931 tungsten carbide cutter. Also known as carbide Kutzall cutters, they're covered with tiny structured carbide burrs, come in several configurations, and are by far the fastest and best cutters I've found. They can be cleaned and rejuvenated by simply burning them clean with a small blowtorch. An optional cutter is a #121 acorn- or flame-shaped high-speed steel cutter. With practice, you'll be able to cut from very fine to wide grooves. These cutters come in various sizes and have good life span, but they get dull and they have to be replaced after time. C. #9935 ball-shaped tungsten-carbide cutter. These cutters come in various sizes. This cutter is ⁵⁄₁₆" and it's fine for cutting things like eye sockets. It will remove wood very quickly. The optional cutter shown is #192, a ³⁄₁₆"-diameter high-speed steel cutter. Available down to ¹⁄₁₆" diameter, these are very good cutters when the round shape is needed. D. #952 grinding stone. I use stones to put the final smooth sanding on tight areas, such as carved faces. Properly used, they will get into areas that sandpaper won't reach; they won't remove a lot of wood and detail. The optional stone shown is #953. It's for the same application, but it's smaller, for tighter areas. It's available in several different configurations.*

2
Craft-Shop Items

All of the craft-shop items pictured in Illus. 2-1 will be discussed in the text, and they can be found in some of the photographs that follow throughout the text. I will try to briefly describe them well enough so that you can accurately describe them to a shopkeeper. I've deliberately used common craft-shop items rather than search for exotic pieces that have to be ordered from specialty catalogs. All of the items listed can be ordered from a shopkeeper's catalogs (if he doesn't have the items in stock), although most items should be in stock at a good store. Some items may be found in hobby shops or in woodworking stores. Browse through such shops, and you'll undoubtedly find other items that could be used.

1. Wood dowels. ⅛″, ³⁄₁₆″, ¼″ diameter.
2. Bamboo food skewers. Available at nearly any supermarket, these skewers come in packages, and they vary in diameter. Most are ³⁄₃₂″ diameter, but I have at least one package that's slightly smaller. These skewers are extremely handy around a shop. I've used them for several years for joining or repairing carved arms, legs, and other parts. They're great for attaching feet to bases, etc.
3. Known as "bean pots," these wooden items make great clown hats.
4. Plastic top hats are available in several sizes.
5. Rubber doll heads.
6. 4mm glass animal eyes come in various sizes and colors.
7. Round wooden doll heads.
8. Wooden thimbles make good comic hats.

9. Tacks come in various colors. Red tacks make the best clown noses.

10. Round wooden balls come in your choice of diameters, some with necks already attached for making doll heads.

11. Pom-poms are round, furry balls that come in nearly any size or color imaginable.

12. Silk roses come in all sizes and colors.

13. Wooden acorns. Sand down the stem area flat and hollow out the acorns to fit the head, using a #9935 round cutter.

14. Wooden beads make great clown noses, and they're available in several sizes.

15. Wooden eggs are available in several sizes.

16. Musical instruments may be the hardest of the objects to find in the sizes you want. The ones I used were all Christmas ornaments. If he doesn't have these objects in stock, ask your shopkeeper to look in the Christmas decorations section of his suppliers' catalogs.

17. Doll hands and arms will be available in any craft store that has a doll section. Such parts come in various sizes and shapes, and they come in pairs. Some shops may also have what they call clown feet and clown hands, but the ones I've seen in stock were too large to use.

18. Chenille bumps are made of fine wire wrapped in various colors of chenille. The wire is about 8″ long, and it can be cut to size and used for the hair on bald clowns, or under the edge of hats to look like hair sticking out from under the hat. These bumps are also used to make scarves on several of my clowns.

Illus. 2-1. *All of the craft-shop items described in this chapter are shown in this photo. The glass animal eyes, the silk roses, the tacks, and the pom-poms, are all very small. The chenille hair is at the far right.*

3
Determining Scale

Model clowns, like humans, are made up of four basic parts. The torso, arms, legs, and heads are common to all humans, but it's the relative size and position of these parts that make the individual. The reason we enjoy watching clowns is that they make a concerted effort to accentuate their body parts by exaggerating the size and position of these as well as their facial expressions.

The patterns you'll find in the following chapters make it simple to change the body-part positions to amusing contortions. The methods used to make the heads and faces are designed for all model builders, novice or advanced.

Before you try to make a clown, decide on the scale you plan to use. I built my first clowns (and all since) to the scale of ¾″ = 1′, and I used the scale of 1″ = 1′ to build horses and wagons.

After visiting model shops, model shows, and reading books and magazines, I became confused by the terms used to describe the various scales. When asked in which scale he builds, the experienced builder answers "O," "HO," or "G," etc. When I asked how these scales converted to inches, those I spoke with gave me proportions ("O" is 1:48). These are common and understandable terms to the experienced model maker, but a woodworker wants to know how many inches equal one foot.

Illus. 3-1 shows the most common scales used in model railroading and it gives the corresponding inches per foot. The term *large scale* is also commonly used. Generally speaking, *large scale* items are trains and accessories made in ⅟₃₂ scale (⅜″ = 1′) or larger. In this book I only describe *large scale* for two reasons. First, the majority of "model peo-

Illus. 3-1. *Here are the most common scales used in model railroading.*

SCALE	EQUIVALENTS	PROPORTION
G	½″ = 1 ft.	1:24
1	⅜″ = 1 ft.	1:32
O	¼″ = 1 ft.	1:48
S	³⁄₁₆″ = 1 ft.	1:64
HO	3.5mm = 1 ft.	1:87.1
TT	⅒″ = 1 ft.	1:120
N	1.9mm = 1 ft.	1:160
Z	1.38mm = 1 ft.	1:220

ple" use smaller scales such as "O" and "HO," and completed manufactured models and parts are readily available to them. The second reason is that working in the smaller scales would be very difficult for most carvers and sculptors. If you have the desire and ability to work in miniature the patterns and plans could be reduced to your scale very easily by most commercial photocopiers. Illus. 3-2 shows the relative height of a 6′-tall clown at various scales. This illustration will show you the very tiny size of the smaller scales. A 6′ clown in "HO" scale would only be 0.84″ tall. Illus. 3-2 also shows how the three clowns on the left (¾″ = 1′, ⅝″ = 1′, ½″ = 1′) could be interchanged in the same setting without looking out of proportion.

All of the clowns shown in the photographs in this book have been made in the ¾″ = 1′ scale. However, the patterns for the body, arms, and legs will show (for your convenience) the other two scales. To make your clowns even more interesting, you could interchange the size of the bodies, legs, and arms. The heads should be made to fit the body size of your clowns, but remember that these are *clowns*, and the more preposterous they look, the funnier they'll be. Illus. 3-3 converts the prototype dimensions to the three scales. This chart should be helpful when you plan your bandwagon or other display materials.

| ¾″ = 1′ | ⅝″ = 1′ | ½″ = 1′
*(G) | ⅜″ = 1′
*(1) | ¼″ = 1′
*(O) |

Illus. 3-2. *Relative height of a 6′-tall clown at various scales. *Model railroad scales. HO man would be 0.84″ tall.*

Illus. 3-3. *This conversion table is for the three larger scales.*

CONVERSION TABLE

PROTOTYPE	½″ = 1′	*⅝″ = 1′	¾″ = 1′
6″	¼″	⁵⁄₁₆″	⅜″
1′	½″	⅝″	¾″
1½′	¾″	1″	1⅛″
2′	1″	1¼″	1½″
3′	1½″	1⅞″	2¼″
4′	2″	2½″	3″
5′	2½″	3⅛″	3¾″
6′	3″	3¾″	4½″
7′	3½″	4⅜″	5¼″
8′	4″	5″	6″
9′	4½″	5⅝″	6¾″
10′	5″	6¼″	7½″
15′	7½″	9⅜″	11¼″
20′	10″	12½″	15″
24′	12″	15″	18″
30′	15″	18¾″	22½″
36′	18″	22½″	27″

*rounded to ⅛

4
Making Clown Bodies

Illustrations 4-1 through 4-8 are the patterns for your clown's body, legs, and arms. These patterns are shown in the three scales previously mentioned, so be sure to choose the correct scale you've selected. The pattern shown on the far right in Illus. 4-1 is for a clown body with a coattail. The other four bodies are interchangeable, and, as you'll notice throughout the photographs in the book, they can be used to make your clown lean, either forward or backwards. I like the bodies that are cut from ½"-thick boards the best, but I use some that are ¾" thick for variation. I usually trace the body on one board and then use double-sided carpet tape to add three more boards before I use a band saw to cut them out. This gives me four bodies to choose from. Drill the dowel holes as shown.

Select the legs and arms you're going to use and saw them with your scroll saw or band saw. Make extras by using the double-sided tape. These parts use very little lumber, so don't be afraid to make too many. When you start to assemble the bodies, you'll have fun deciding which arms and legs look the best.

Basswood is by far the nicest wood to work with, but other clear lumber will work. You'll need boards ¾", ½", and ¼" thick. You can buy the ¼" boards in most hobby shops, but doing so is far more expensive than using ¾" material and planing it down. If you don't have a surface planer, most lumber dealers will plane the wood for you. The following photographs show the step-by-step procedure for assembling

Illus. 4-1. *Body patterns. Cut the patterns from ½"-thick wood (¾" for "fat" clowns).*

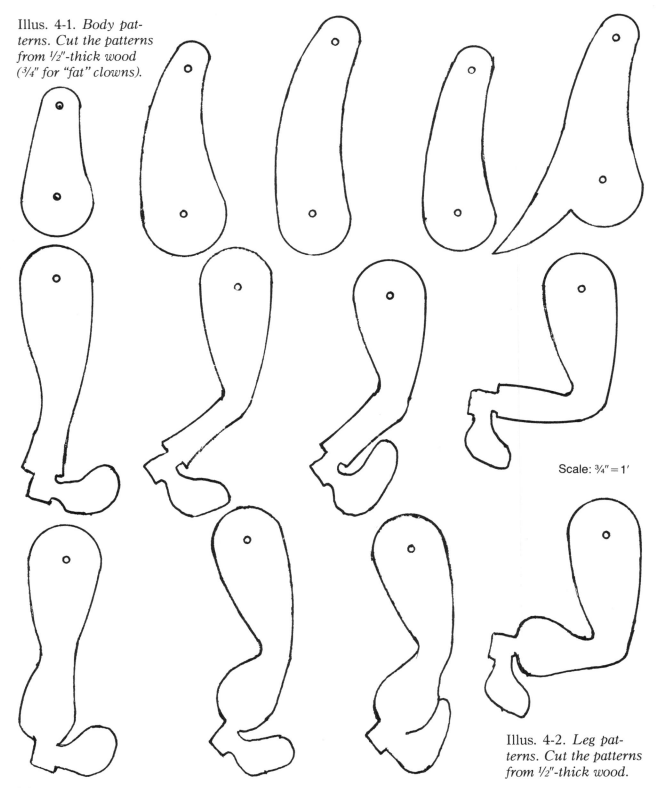

Scale: ¾" = 1'

Illus. 4-2. *Leg patterns. Cut the patterns from ½"-thick wood.*

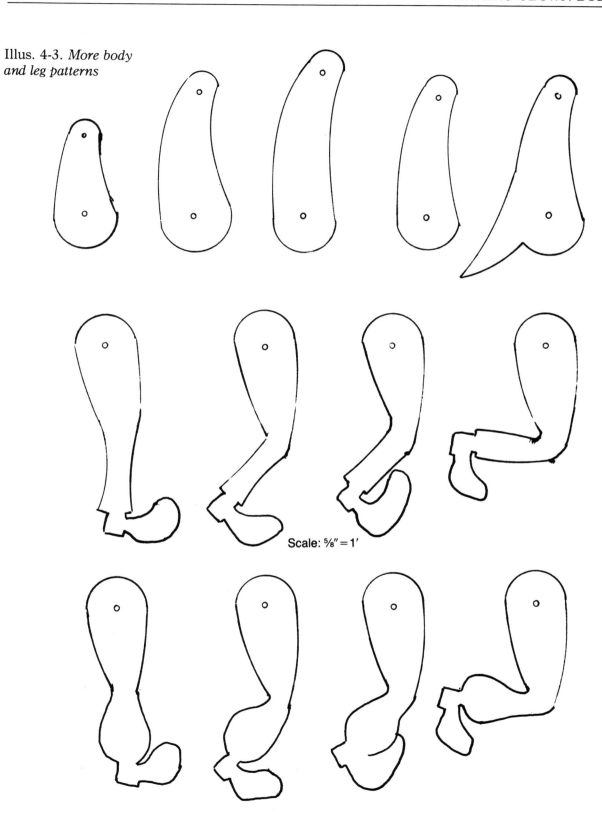

Illus. 4-3. *More body
and leg patterns*

Scale: ⅝" = 1'

Illus. 4-4. *More body and leg patterns*

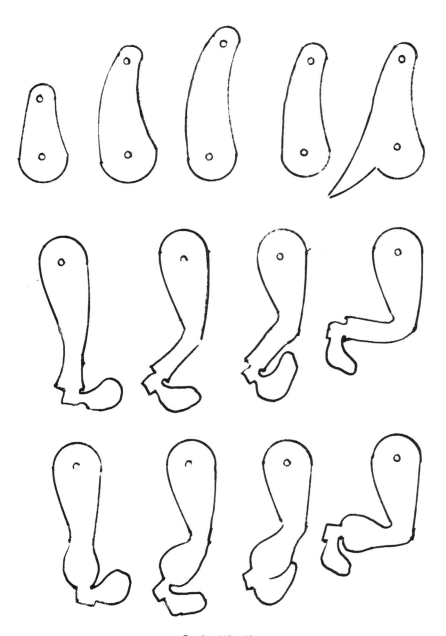

Scale: ½"=1'

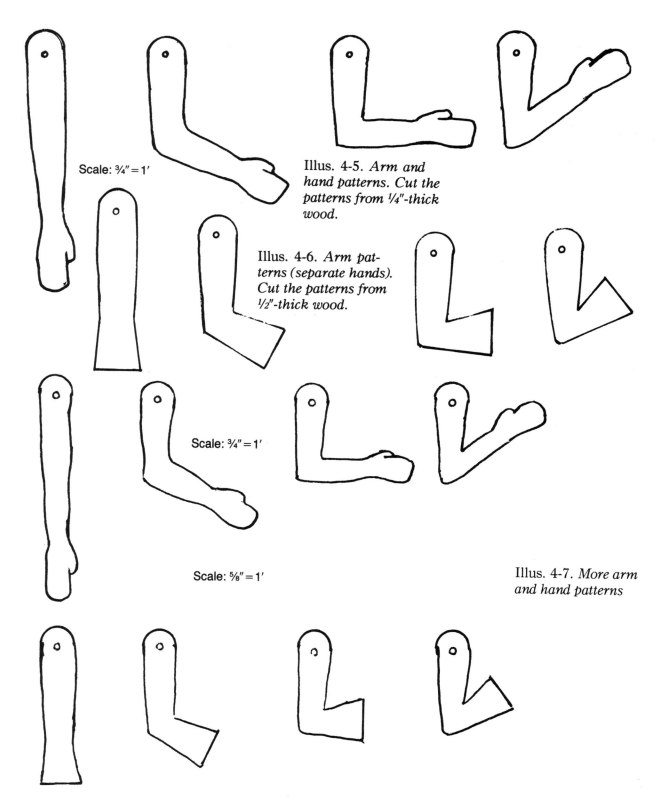

Scale: ¾" = 1'

Illus. 4-5. *Arm and hand patterns. Cut the patterns from ¼"-thick wood.*

Illus. 4-6. *Arm patterns (separate hands). Cut the patterns from ½"-thick wood.*

Scale: ¾" = 1'

Scale: ⅝" = 1'

Illus. 4-7. *More arm and hand patterns*

Illus. 4-8. *Choose, cut, and sand the arm you chose. If you use the flared cuff, sand a dowel to fit the hand, drill a hole that size in the arm about ³/₄" deep, and then drill a larger hole for the wrist to fit in. If you use the other arm, simply cut and sand the end of the arm to fit the doll hand. When glued in place and painted, you can put on a "glitter" cuff (see the chapter on painting) to cover the connection.*

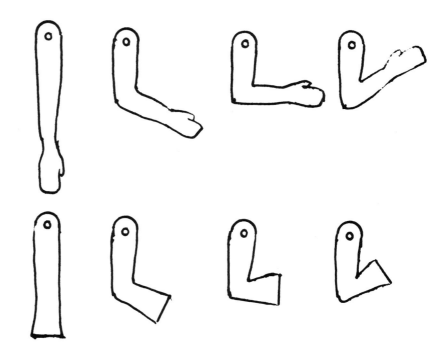

Illus. 4-9. *These rubber doll hands can be purchased at craft shops, and they can be easily adapted for use with your clowns.*

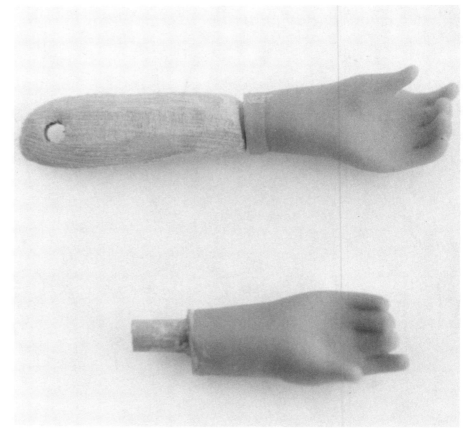

the bodies. The body shown in the following photos will be a policeman, as you'll see.

If you can't really carve the hands, you might want to go to a craft shop and buy some rubber doll hands; these hands come in various sizes and shapes and they're simple to adapt to your clowns. Follow the directions under Illus. 4-9.

Illustrations 4-10 through 4-31 show all the steps needed to carve the clowns' bodies.

Caution: Don't flatten and angle the upper arm to fit the body until you've determined the angle at which you want the arm to extend from the body. If you look through the photos in this book, you'll see that by properly sanding the arm you can put it in any position you want.

Study the clowns pictured in Illustrations 4-32 through 4-54 on pages 40–53, and you will realize the endless combinations of bodies, legs, and arms. With just these few patterns and your imagination, you can make as many clowns as you could ever want, and never have a duplicate.

Illus. 4-10. *The ½" sanding drum and pointed Kutzall cutter (#9931) were the only cutters I used to make this body. I have other cutters that could have been used but I used these two to show that it doesn't take a lot of equipment to make clown bodies.*

Illus. 4-11. *Drill the dowel holes as shown. You can use ⅛" dowels, but I prefer to use bamboo food skewers. You can buy these skewers in packages in almost any grocery store, and they're very economical to use. Most of these skewers come in ³/₃₂" diameter, but you can drill these holes to fit your dowels. Glue dowels in the holes in the body and leave a short (⅛" or even less) protrusion on both sides. Put the arms and legs on the body before gluing them, to determine right and left, and mark them as shown.*

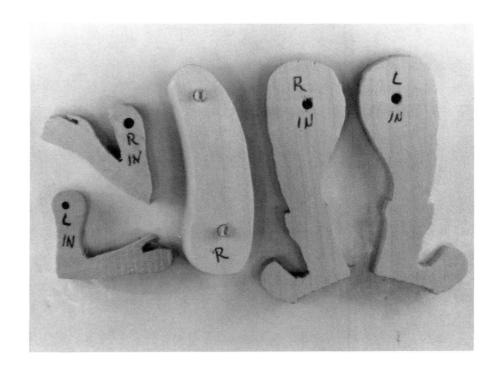

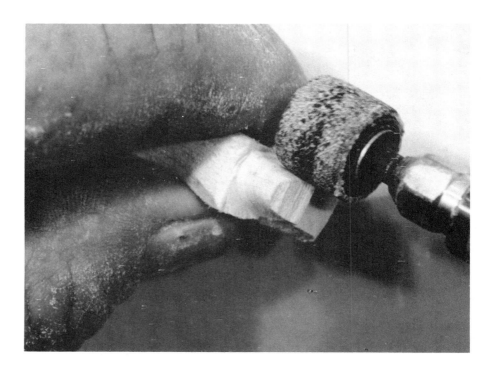

Illus. 4-12. *Start by shaping the heel.*

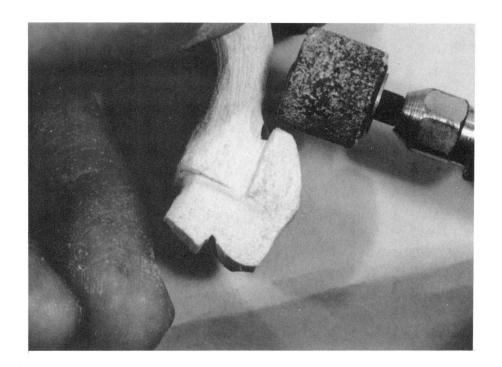

Illus. 4-13. *Round the toe and taper down to the heel.*

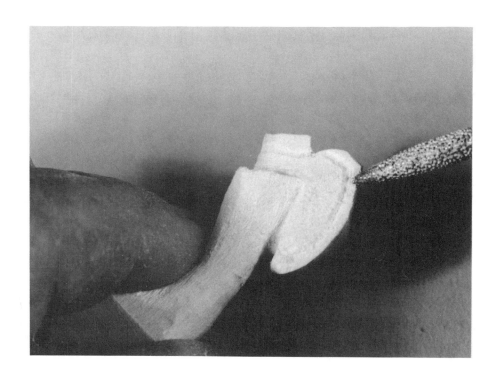

Illus. 4-14. *Form the heel and sole.*

Illus. 4-15. *Sand the lower leg round. Sand the hip round on the outside only. Use a disc sander or belt sander to angle the inside of the leg where it joins the body. Vary this angle until you have the leg going out from the body at the angle you want.*

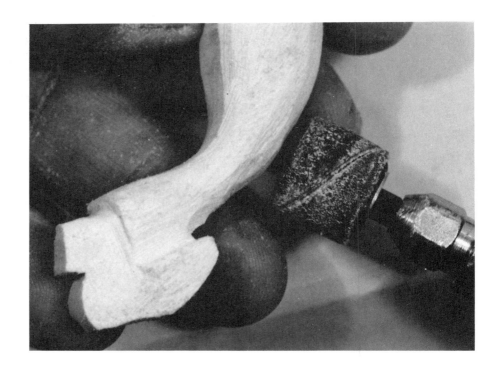

Illus. 4-16. *Assemble the legs to the body before gluing them, and mark their positions on the body for reference while gluing them. Notice that the inside of the hips has been angled as in Illus. 4-11 above. This is a normal fit for the legs to the body.*

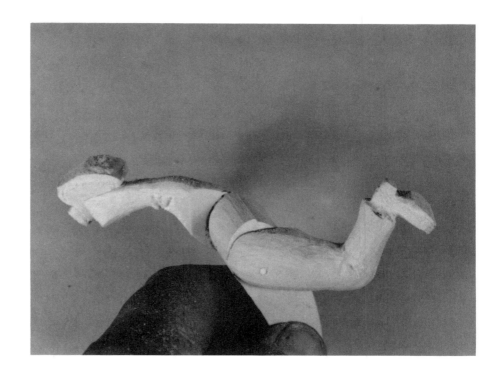

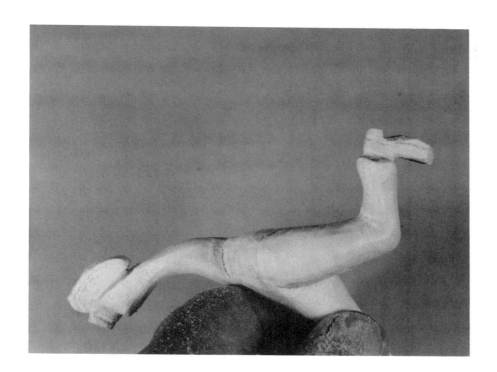

Illus. 4-17. *Use the drum sander to shape the body to the legs.*

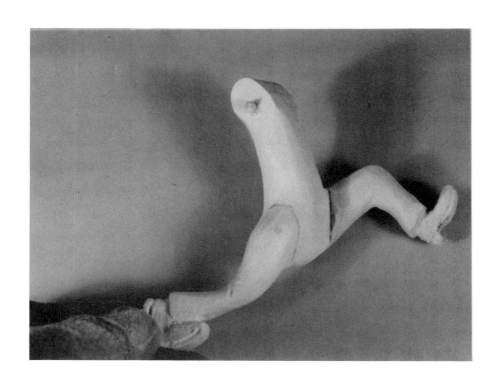

Illus. 4-18. *The legs are on. The body has been rounded up to the shoulder area.*

Illus. 4-19. *Choose the arms you want to use. Hold them on the body in the position you want and mark the arms left and right, in and out, so that you'll know which way the thumb and fingers go, and how to sand the upper arm. Drill a dowel-size hole and sand off as much wood as the drum sander shown can reach.*

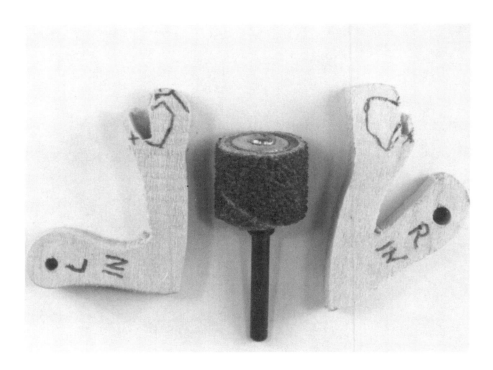

Illus. 4-20. *Enlarge the hole and complete the shaping with the pointed cutter shown. The next three photos show more details on carving the hands.*

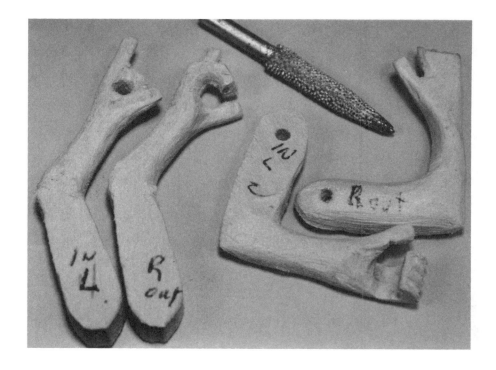

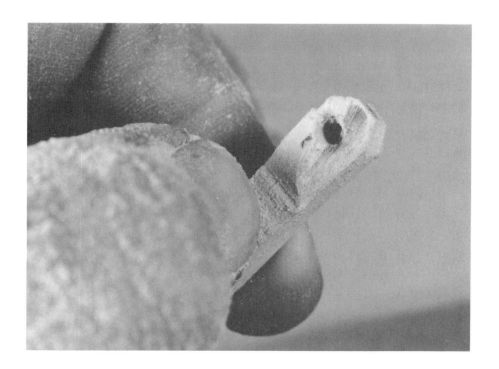

Illus. 4-21. *Determine the direction you want the hand to open and drill a small hole (same size as the dowel hole above) through the hand in the direction you want. Flatten the outside of the hand as shown.*

Illus. 4-22. *Use the pointed Kutzall cutter to enlarge the hole until the finger thickness is correct. Shape the wrist and thumb.*

Illus. 4-23. *Shape the palm and make the lines between the fingers using the pointed cutter.*

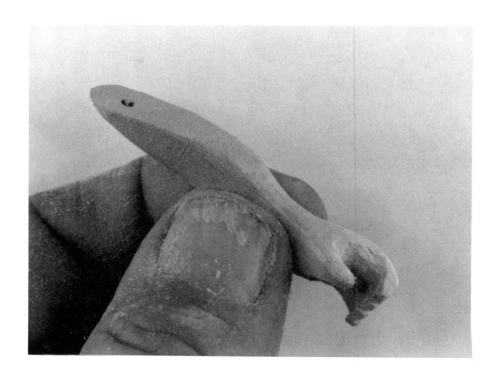

Illus. 4-24. *Round the arm up to the shoulder area. Angle the inside of the upper arm until it protrudes at the angle you want, as shown.*

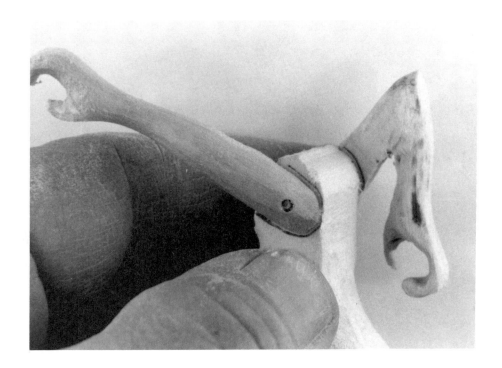

Illus. 4-25. *A normal fit for the arms to the body while being clamped to glue. Note the pencil mark I made on the body when I determined the arm angle I wanted.*

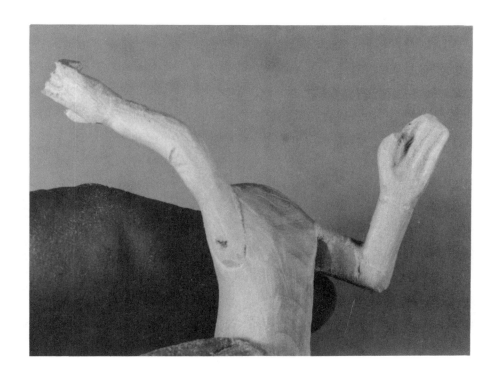

Illus. 4-26. *Use the drum sander to blend the body to the arms.*

Illus. 4-27. *This step is optional; I draw the coat and lapels in pencil.*

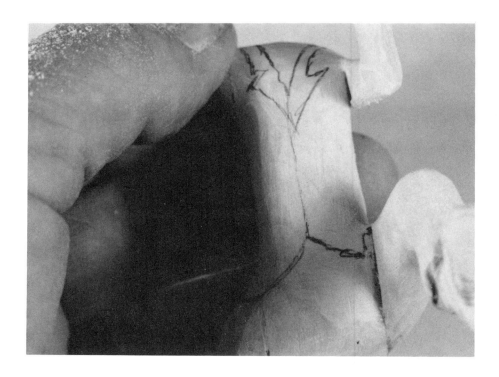

Illus. 4-28. *Use the pointed cutter to accentuate the coat outlines and to round the areas of the legs and arms that the drum sander didn't reach.*

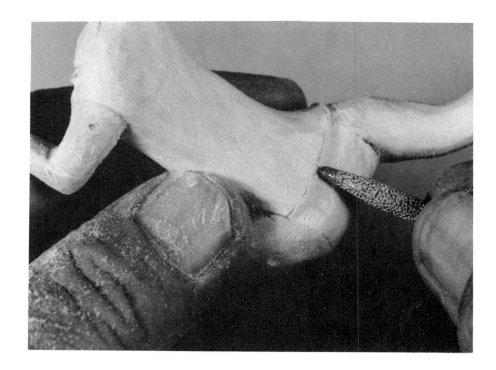

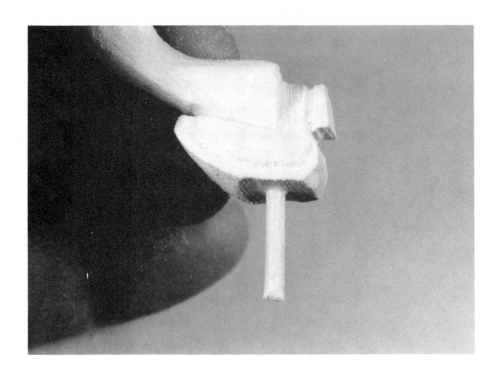

Illus. 4-29. *Glue a dowel in the foot where the foot will touch the ground.*

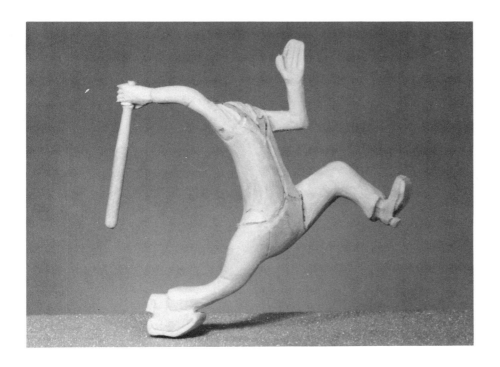

Illus. 4-30. *Shape the billy club from a 3/16" dowel and glue it in place. Sand down the figure and he's ready for paint. Paint him before you put on the head.*

41

Illus. 4-31. *Here's your cop. He has an egg head, an acorn hat, a blue uniform, and his star. Now he's ready to chase the tramp in the big parade.*

Illus. 4-32. *The bodies of the driver and the brakeman were cut from ¾" wood and they were then sanded narrow in the areas where the legs were attached. After the legs were glued in place, the voids were filled with wood filler. This gives the appearance of an overhanging coat. This process can be done wherever the legs will protrude forward as shown.*

Illus. 4-33. *Here's a rear view of the over-hanging coat.*

Illus. 4-34. *Lighting the fuse*

Illus. 4-35. *A long-strided sprint*

Illus. 4-36. *Part of the high-wire act?*

Illus. 4-37. *The high strutter*

Illus. 4-38. *The janitor*

Illus. 4-39. *Note the bold polka dots.*

Illus. 4-40. *Note the plastic parasol.*

Illus. 4-41. *The bare-back rider*

Illus. 4-42. *Close-up of the bareback rider*

Illus. 4-43. *The trapeze act*

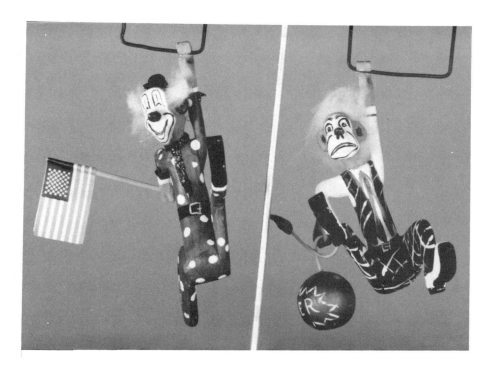

Illus. 4-44. *The band-wagon's driver*

Illus. 4-45. *The band-wagon's brakeman*

Illus. 4-46. *A horn player*

Illus. 4-47. *The drummer*

Illus. 4-48. *Another horn player*

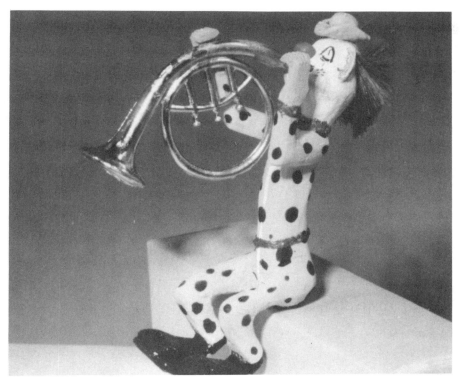

Illus. 4-49. *Yet another horn player*

Illus. 4-50. *Another member of the brass section*

Illus. 4-51. *Another*

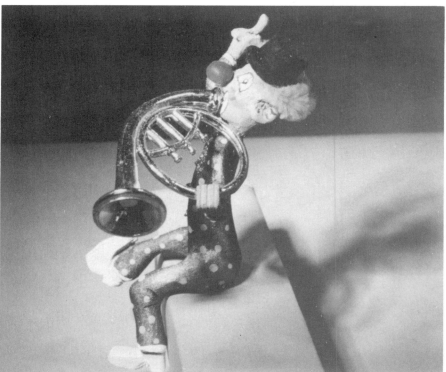

Illus. 4-52. *And yet another*

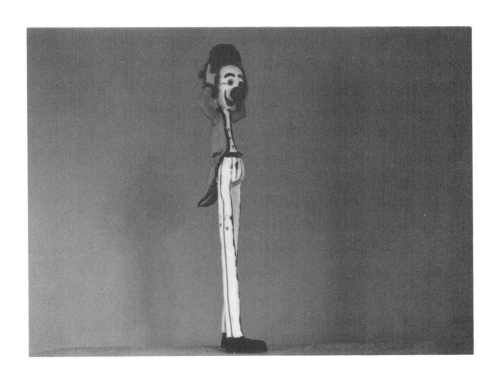

Illus. 4-53. *Clown on stilts*

Illus. 4-54. *The beginning of the circus parade*

5
Heads and Faces

There's nothing more individual than the human face. Each face has the same parts: eyes, nose, mouth, brow, hairline, chin, hair, and ears. The size, color, and relative location of these parts make each of us completely different and completely individual.

Professional clowns attend seminars to learn to apply makeup that will accentuate their personal features. Clowns make every effort to make their faces individual, and these faces become their personal "trademark." This individuality is great for the model maker, because it means that he has complete freedom to make his clowns look any way that he wishes. There are no face patterns shown in this book, so the design of the face you make can't be wrong!

Let's begin this chapter with the premise that the clowns you make and the looks they have are your own creations, and not just copies.

Each artist has his own talents. In this chapter I'll try to deal with varying talents by showing how to carve a face, sculpt a face, and how to use simple, readily available craft- and art-shop supplies. I feel that the "average" woodworker can make the bodies for these clowns with just a few simple tools. Likewise, I believe the "average" crafts person can make good clown faces by following a few simple steps.

Illus. 5-1 shows some basic guidelines that will apply to all of the faces in this chapter. You will see that the "normal" face is divided into four equal distances formed by the hairline, eyebrow, nose, and chin. Normally the distance from the eyebrow to the chin is equal to the distance from the point of the chin to the ear. The horizontal eye line is generally in the center of the face. Not illustrated by this photo is the fact that the height of the head is normally $\frac{1}{7}$ of the

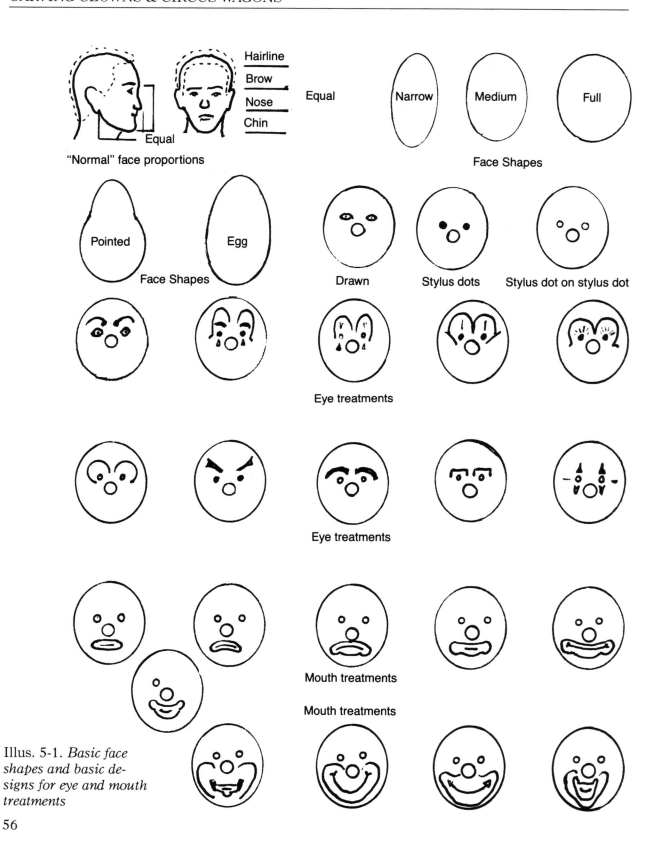

Illus. 5-1. *Basic face shapes and basic designs for eye and mouth treatments*

body's total height. With simple mathematics and/or the conversion tables shown in Illus. 3-3 on page 24, you can easily find the correct height for your clown's head. Remember that you don't have to be perfect with these dimensions. These clowns are caricatures, and they'll be more amusing if they're slightly out of normal proportions. Illus. 5-1 shows five basic face shapes. These shapes will be discussed later.

I make the clown's eyes either by painting a real eye or by using a stylus to make a black dot for an eye. Most styluses have two sizes of balls; on many of the clown faces I make a large black dot and then a small white dot on top of the black dot when the first dot is dry. If you are an accomplished wood-carver, you'll want to carve the clown's eyes.

Illus. 5-1 also includes a few basic designs which clowns use for eye and mouth treatments. You can mix and match these designs to vary your faces. You'll find variations of these and other designs in the photos throughout the book.

There are three basic clown types: *whiteface, auguste,* and *tramp.* The whitefaces have a white base coat, and they can be *neat whitefaces* with only simple black and red accents or *comedy whitefaces,* with larger and bolder accents in almost any color. The base coat for the auguste clown is either flesh color or pink color, and white is only used to accent the eyes and mouth. The auguste clown uses bright colors, outlandish features, false noses, and wigs to complete his makeup. The tramp clown normally has a dark beard, large white mouth, rosy cheeks, a red nose, and white around his eyes. The tramp can be either a *happy tramp* or a *traditional tramp,* depending mostly on his mouth shape. You will see these three types of faces in the photos found in this book.

Power-Tool-Carving the Clown Face

I carve with power tools such as the Dremel moto-tool, so let's start by explaining that method. The tools and cutters used to carve these faces are discussed in chapter 1. Study the tool section to understand the captions under Illustrations 5-2 through 5-7.

Sculpting the Head

My favorite way to make a clown head is with modelling compound (sometimes called artificial clay). It's available in hobby shops, art-supply stores, craft shops, catalogs, and elsewhere. The two brands I use are shown in Illus. 5-8. I'm sure that there are other brands. This compound is easy to work with, and it can be easily changed. When completed, you just place the head in your kitchen oven for 30 minutes at 300 °F. The heads won't shrink, and they come out hard and permanent. They can be drilled, carved, sanded, and they can even be added to and returned to the oven as many times as you wish. The modelling material comes in sticks, and this helps you measure the amount you're using. Illustrations 5-9, 5-10, and 5-11 show some easy steps to follow.

After the head is baked and cooled, any imperfections can be removed or details added by using your power-tool carving equipment. The head can be cut almost like wood.

If you want to add a hat (or any other addition), you can sculpt and attach it and put the heads right back in the oven. I've left some figures in the oven by mistake for over three hours, and they were undamaged.

Illustrations 5-12 through 5-31, shown on pages 64 through 73 are close-ups of faces which were made from modelling compound. The photos illustrate the wide variations you can achieve by using this material.

Clowns Straight from the Craft Shop!

Illus. 5-32 on page 74 should give you some ideas for your clowns' heads and faces. These doll heads should be available in any craft shop. They are about ¾″ high, and they'd work on any of the three scales you're working with. The clown head on the right is just as it came from the shop. On the left of the photo is a standard girl doll head. (A boy doll head is also available.) As you can see, I just added a tack nose, painted the eyes and mouth, and added a craft-shop

Illus. 5-2. *Cut a piece of wood 1" square about 3" to 4" long. Round the top and mark the hair, brow, nose, and chin lines, and the ear locations as shown. Sand the neck down to round and use the #9935 round cutter to make the eye sockets and mouth areas.*

Illus. 5-3. *Use a #407 drum sander to define the ears and round the back of the head. Taper the head down to the neck. Define the chin and jaw lines.*

Illus. 5-4. *Use the #9931 pointed carbide cutter (or an optional one) to clean out the ears, shape the nose, the mouth line, and the chin.*

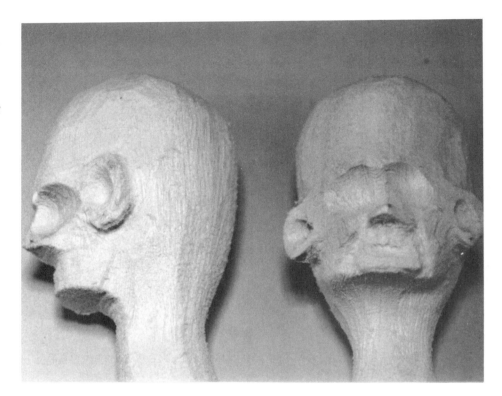

Illus. 5-5. *Use the drum sander to lower the top of the head to the proportion you want. You can carve the hair in place with the pointed cutter (as shown on the left), or you could leave the head bald, so that hair can be added later.*

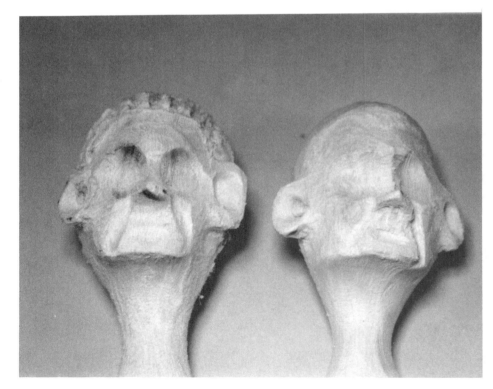

Illus. 5-6. *The finished and painted faces*

Illus. 5-7. *The hair has been carved and painted on the clown on the left. The hair on the other clown is real horsehair glued in place to stand up straight, leaving the clown bald on top.*

Illus. 5-8. *Two brands of plastic compounds used as clay substitutes*

Illus. 5-9. *Start by sanding the end of a dowel (the size you want for your neck—¼"—is shown) to a shape similar to the one shown in the photo. Flatten the surfaces to help hold the dowel in place inside the compound. I used two sticks of modelling compound for this head. Roll the modelling compound into a ball and insert the dowel. The three steps, shown from the left, are:*

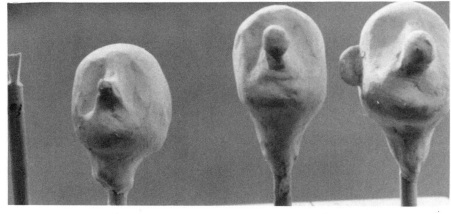

(1) With your thumbs, press the eye sockets and mouth areas, leaving material for the nose. With the end of your finger, push material down to the neck. (2) Remove excess material from the nose and form a ball, as shown. Use about ½" off the end of a round toothpick to attach the ball to the end of the nose. Shape the back and sides of the head by pushing the excess modelling compound downwards to the neck. At this stage, it's very easy to press the head between your thumb and forefinger to give the head the shape you want—narrow, medium, or full. (3) Form flat pieces in the shape of ears and attach them to the head by using the end of a round toothpick or a bamboo food skewer.

Illus. 5-10. *Profiles of the three steps*

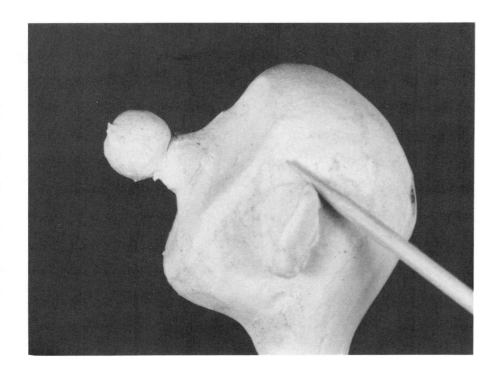

Illus. 5-11. *Close-up of the head showing the point of a bamboo food skewer (or the end of a round toothpick) used to attach the ears to the head. A wooden stick of this type will roll out imperfections you want removed. Don't be concerned with small imperfections like the ones seen around the nose.*

Illus. 5-12. *Close-up of a clown face made from modelling compound*

Illus. 5-13. *A clown face made from modelling compound*

The collection of clowns on the right includes a bareback rider, a clown on stilts and the cop. Below is a view of the bandwagon taken from above. The driver, the brakeman, and the horn section are all clearly shown.

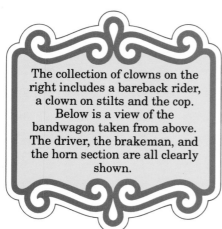

B

Here's the complete circus parade. Note the beautifully carved draft horses, the detailed bandwagon, and the fabulous collection of clowns. Creating a piece such as this would ensure the reputation of any amateur craftsperson!

C

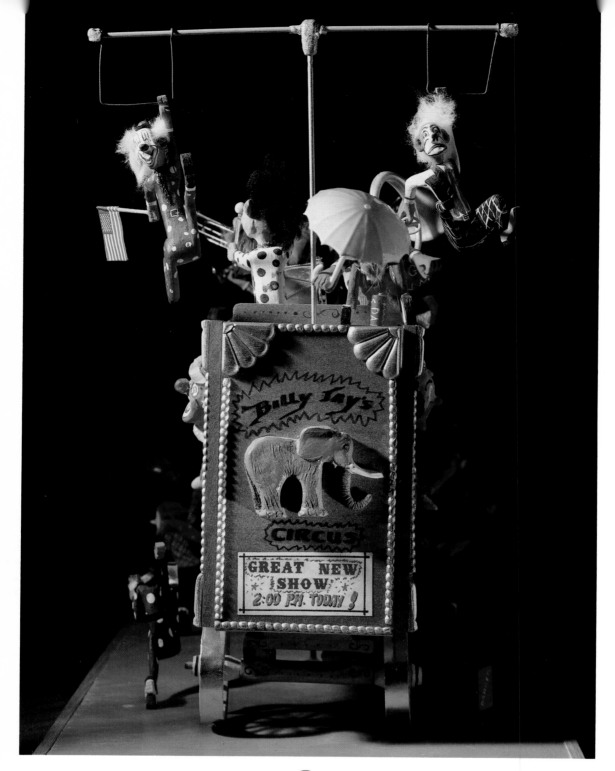

The back end of the bandwagon. This photo shows the construction of the bandwagon, especially the rear axle. Visible also are the two trapeze artists, the rear display panel, and some of the members of the clown's brass band.

Illus. 5-14. *Another clown face made from modelling compound*

Illus. 5-15. *One more clown face made from modelling compound*

Illus. 5-16. *Yet another clown face made from modelling compound*

Illus. 5-17. *Another clown face made from modelling compound*

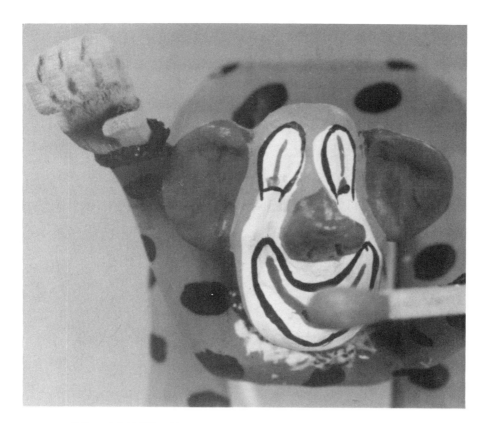

Illus. 5-18. *Clown face made from modelling compound*

Illus. 5-19. *Detail of a clown face made from modelling compound*

Illus. 5-20. *Detail of a clown face made from modelling compound*

Illus. 5-21. *Clown face made from modelling compound*

Illus. 5-22. *Clown face made from modelling compound*

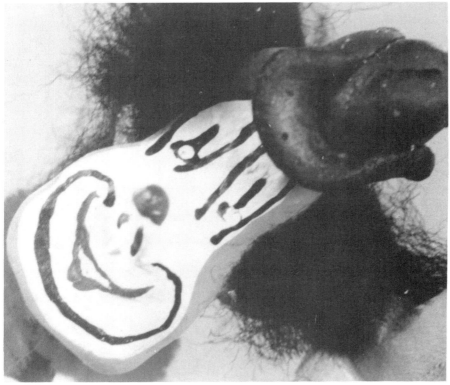

Illus. 5-23. *Clown face made from modelling compound*

Illus. 5-24. *Detail of a clown face made from modelling compound*

Illus. 5-25. *Clown face made from modelling compound*

Illus. 5-26. *Detail of a clown face made from modelling compound*

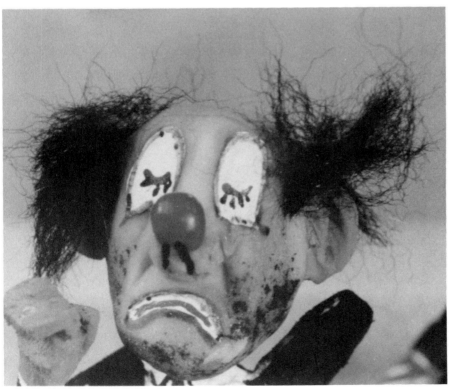

Illus. 5-27. *Close-up of a clown face made from modelling compound*

Illus. 5-28. *Detail of a clown face made from modelling compound*

Illus. 5-29. *Clown face made from modelling compound*

Illus. 5-30. *Detail of the driver's face made from modelling compound*

Illus. 5-31. *The brake-man's face made from modelling compound*

Illus. 5-32. *Clown heads made from doll heads. The doll heads can be found in almost any craft store.*

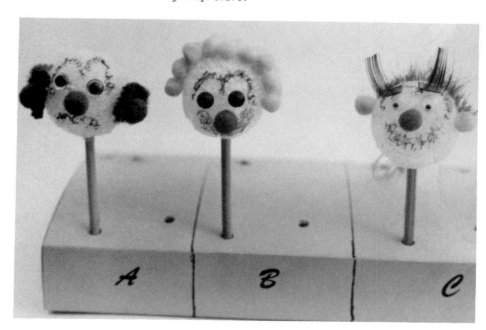

Illus. 5-33. *Simple-to-make clown faces made from Styrofoam® balls*

Illus. 5-34. *Three easy steps for making clown heads from wooden eggs available in most craft shops*

Illus. 5-35. *Another view of the three steps involved in making clown heads from wooden eggs*

Illus. 5-36. *This police-man has painted eyes (stylus dots), wooden-bead nose, tramp mouth, fake-fur red hair, and a wooden acorn hat.*

Illus. 5-37. *This white-face clown has a wooden-egg head, glass eyes, wooden-bead nose, and a 1" green pom-pom for hair.*

Illus. 5-38. *Wooden doll heads, as shown in "A," come painted flesh color and in different sizes. Clown "B" has a dowel neck, tack nose, clown eyes and mouth, a piece of chenille bump for hair, and a wooden thimble for a hat. The hat decorations were painted with a stylus. When you dip the stylus in paint, you'll get about seven progressively smaller dots. The hair is green, the hat is red with white dots. Clown "C" has the same dowel neck, tack nose, and clown face, but it has cotton-ball hair and a wooden "bean pot" hat with a tiny pom-pom on top.*

Illus. 5-39. *A finished clown head made from a wooden doll head*

77

Illus. 5-40. *Another clown head made from a wooden doll head*

hat and made a nice little clown. If heads and faces are difficult for you, this is an easy way to make them. You could color the hair, or remove it, and use any of the hair treatments shown in this book to come up with as many different faces as you want.

Illus. 5-33 is included just to show how simple faces can be. I haven't used any of these faces on the clowns shown in this book, but they may spark an idea that would be useful to you. They are 3/4" Styrofoam balls, also available in many other diameters. Stick a dowel in for a neck. The face on the left has a pom-pom nose, tack eyes, and tiny pom-poms for hair. The middle face has the same eyes and nose, but it has bumpy chenille hair and pom-pom ears. The face on the right has a pom-pom nose (you could use a tack), moveable doll eyes, pom-pom ears, false eyelashes, and fake-fur hair. The mouth and eye treatments were done using a felt-tip pen.

The Egg Head

You don't have to be an artist, sculptor, or wood-carver to make these clown heads. Your craft shop will have wooden eggs in several sizes. The ones used here were 1½″ long. Buy the size you want, but these will work very well for either ½″- or ¾″-scale clowns. Illustrations 5-34 and 5-35 show the three easy steps. The lower head has the point up and the upper has the point down to give you two completely different face shapes. To handle the eggs, make a ball of modelling compound a little larger than a golf ball and press the egg into it and flatten the compound at the bottom. This base will hold the egg at any angle you want it.

Step A: Drill ⅛″ holes for the neck and nose in about the positions shown. You can change the angle of the head and the location of the nose to suit your own taste. Moving the nose up or down will change the look of the clown's face. If you plan to use glass eyes, use the same drill bit to drill the eyeholes. Glue a ⅛″ dowel in place for the neck. Leave about 2″ of the dowel protruding to help you handle the head for the next steps. Cut a dowel for the nose that will protrude about ¼″, but don't glue it in place just yet.

Step B: Paint the head white for a *whiteface* clown or flesh color for an *auguste* clown. Press the head into the modelling compound to hold the head in place as you paint. Choose mouth and eye designs from the ones shown on page 56, and draw them in with a pencil. Paint them the colors that you choose and outline the mouth and eye areas with a permanent-ink felt-tip pen. These outline borders can cover any painting errors.

Step C: Glue the ⅛″ dowel in place for the nose. If you choose, this dowel can be shortened and painted for the nose. I used ¼″ wooden beads for the noses. Fill the nose hole with wood filler and press the bead in place. Wipe off the excess fill smooth. You might paint the nose red before putting it in place, and then just touch-paint the wood filler. If you use 4mm glass eyes, fill the eye holes with wood filler before pressing the eyes into place. Decide which hair design you want. I used 1″ pom-poms for the wigs on the clowns shown in Illustrations 5-34 and 5-35. Cover the hair area with glue, cut the pom-pom about halfway through with scissors, spread it out, and press it into the glue.

The variations, expressions, and looks you can get from these simple and common craft-shop items are unlimited! Illustrations 5-36 and 5-37 show two finished egg-head clowns.

The clown heads shown in Illus. 5-38 are made completely from craft-shop materials. They're easy and simple to make. Any craft shop should have parts; you supply the paints. Easy-to-make and cute little clown faces are shown in Illustrations 5-39 and 5-40.

Clown Wigs

A clown without a wig would never be allowed in a parade or under the big top. He may be made up to be bald or often a clean whiteface clown has his hair covered to appear bald. Each clown's wig seems to be different—different shape, texture, and color. This is great for the clown model maker; he can't make a mistake because there is no "right" wig. All kinds of wigs are pictured on the clowns shown throughout this book. Here are some brief descriptions and names for the things I use to make wigs:

Human hair. Use your children's or your grandchildren's hair; you'll get a very favorable response from them. If you make a clown to give to a friend, ask his barber to save you some hair the next time the friend goes for a haircut.

Horsehair. It is very coarse and unruly.

Cotton balls. Cotton balls can be dyed to whatever color you want; they make great white hair and they're easy to work with.

Discarded women's wigs. Get them for a song at garage sales.

Craft-shop pom-poms. These are colorful, easy to work with, and they come in different sizes. Small 4mm ones packed tightly on the head make the wig look curly.

Craft-shop curly hair. A small package has enough to make hundreds of model clowns.

Mock wool (sometimes called "folk wool"). Mock wool comes in rope form and in different colors. A small package goes a long way.

Fake fur. This usually comes in pads about 6″ × 12″, and in many wild colors. Just cut off as much hair as you need.

Dog hair. Snip some as Fido snoozes.

Wig samples. If you know a beautician, he or she will have a set of wig samples, usually about 24 assorted colors in a set. Any of the colors will make great wigs. I use them for the manes on small carousel horses.

To apply the hair, simply cover the area with a thick coat of a good glue and put the hair in place. You can make the hair stand up or lay down in any position you want. The pictures throughout this book show hair ideas.

6
Painting & Finishing

Possibly the most critical, important, difficult, and time-consuming parts of making an attractive clown are painting and finishing; but they are also the most rewarding steps. Your clown really comes to life as you apply color to him. Painting may be my favorite part of most projects. You don't have to be an accomplished artist or painter to derive much satisfaction from painting and finishing. I can only offer some tips on the painting equipment I use and how I use it.

Paints

I use regular hardware-store spray paint for a base coat on large areas. Others have told me that a sealer coat should be used before painting, and I sometimes do, but it seems to me that two coats of the same color accomplish the same thing. I use Krylon acrylic sealer when I do use a sealer. It dries almost instantly. I always use a sealer when I'm "antiquing" a carving (not clowns). If you don't seal the sanded-off "worn" spots, the antique stain will penetrate the wood and the color will be too dark.

I use two-ounce and eight-ounce plastic bottles of acrylic paint, the kind with the flip-top lids. I use permanent-ink felt-tip pens whenever I can. I can make very straight lines with these. Be sure the ink is permanent and let the ink dry if you're going to spray a sealer or varnish over the finished object.

I discovered "glitter writers" several years ago. I used them originally (and still do) to decorate miniature carousel horses, but they're even better for trimming and finishing clowns. They come in one-ounce tubes in a wide range of colors. Instructions printed on the tubes tell you how to apply the glitter (it's just like writing with a pen), and the tube leaves a three-dimensional bead of glitter that's perfect for collars, cuffs, coat trim, etc. You'll see this glitter on most of the clowns pictured in this book. The glitter dries overnight. It's easily smeared when you first apply it, but it's permanent when dry.

I give many of my carvings a clear coat of varnish after they're painted and dried, and they've set for a few days.

Brushes

I buy medium-priced brushes, and they seem to be adequate. After ruining several brushes, I've learned to have a glass of water and a paper towel ready to clean my brush immediately after I finish using it. Because the paints I use dry so fast, a brush can be ruined after its first use if it isn't cleaned at once.

To paint very fine lines, I use an "O" liner brush and thin the paint to the texture of ink. I use #1, #2, and #4 brushes (both round and flat) wherever they fit my need. I have a #12 flat brush for larger areas and a feather brush.

One of my most-used "brushes" is a two-pointed stylus. These styluses are available anywhere brushes are sold. They're perfect for making small dots for things like eyes, or buttons. I also use them for making designs on hats. One dip in paint will make about seven progressively smaller dots.

When I need larger dots, I just use a short piece of wooden dowel. Use a dowel that matches the size dot you need, dip the end in paint and touch it to your clown. You will notice dots all over the clowns pictured.

I often use a rotating sander in my drill press to smooth-sand carvings. I like to spray my first base coat of paint on the project, and then sand it. This gets rid of the grain that rises from the wood when you first paint it. Set your drill press at its slowest speed; don't press your carving into the rotating sander, since the sander can knock the piece out of your hand. The sander can destroy fine details if you use it too much. For tight areas (around horses' heads and legs, for example) I use a homemade wooden bow sander. Shaped like a hacksaw, this sander holds 1"-wide emery cloth and it gets into very tight and delicate areas easily.

7
Building the Bandwagon

I spent far more time planning and thinking about my band-wagon than I spent building it. If you plan to build a band-wagon, this chapter could save you a lot of time. I'll deal only with the one I built. You, of course, may want to change the scale and size or even the design, but I'm sure you'll find ideas here that will help you. This size wagon will work for any of the large-scale clowns we have talked about earlier ($\frac{3}{4}''$, $\frac{5}{8}''$, or $\frac{1}{2}'' = 1'$), but it would be a simple matter to change the size of the wagon. If you want to convert to a dif-ferent scale, use the chart on page 24.

I knew the size I wanted the wagon to be, and I knew that I couldn't carve the sides very well. I had once used some gingerbread wood carvings purchased at a wood-specialty store. Many wood-specialty stores and many catalogs list these carvings. These carvings are used to decorate furni-ture. A long search through many catalogs turned up a carving nearly the size I wanted. I also ordered ten corner carvings and 10' of beaded trim $\frac{3}{16}''$ wide. I think they worked great (with some very minor modifications) and they do resemble the real, beautifully carved circus wagons. You will see all three of these items in the photos of the com-pleted bandwagon.

The wagon is a simple rectangular box made from $\frac{1}{2}''$-thick lumber (you could use $\frac{3}{4}''$) with $\frac{1}{4}''$-thick display panels attached. I made the wagon this way so I could work on the side and end panels individually, and I could remove the panels if they ever needed repairs or changes. When the box was built and the display panels cut, I carefully drilled several ⅛″ dowel holes through the panels and box sides to hold the panels in the proper place when I finally attached them with screws. I glued dowels in the box that protruded out slightly less than ¼″. Illustrations 7-1, 7-2, 7-3, and 7-4 show the four completed display panels.

I sculpted the elephants shown using modelling compound (described on page 58 and shown in Illus. 5-8). Illus. 7-5 shows the patterns I used to make the elephants.

There are four different clown faces on each side panel. Illustrations 7-6 through 7-13 show close-ups of these faces. Illustrations 7-14 and 7-15 show close-ups of the elephant heads.

Illustrations 7-16, 7-17, and 7-18 are the plans and descriptions of the wagon's construction.

Illus. 7-1. *A side view of the completed bandwagon*

Illus. 7-2. *The other side of the bandwagon*

Illus. 7-3. *The bandwagon's rear panel*

Illus. 7-4. *The band-wagon's front panel*

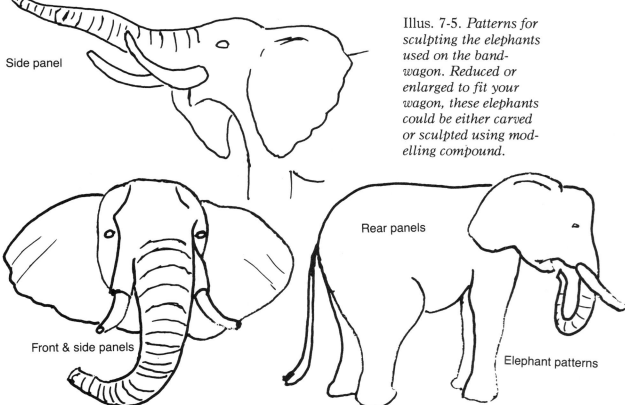

Side panel

Illus. 7-5. *Patterns for sculpting the elephants used on the band-wagon. Reduced or enlarged to fit your wagon, these elephants could be either carved or sculpted using modelling compound.*

Rear panels

Front & side panels

Elephant patterns

Illus. 7-6. *One of the eight clown faces on the bandwagon's side panels*

Illus. 7-7. *Another of the eight clown faces*

Illus. 7-8. *This clown face was made from modelling compound.*

Illus. 7-9. *Yet another of the clown faces from the side panel*

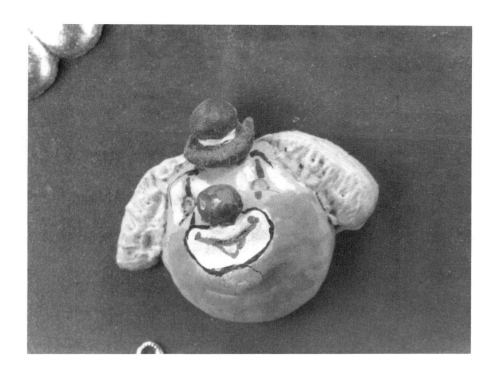

Illus. 7-10. *One of the clown faces on the side panel of the bandwagon*

Illus. 7-11. *One of the clown faces, made from modelling compound*

Illus. 7-12. *Another of the eight clown faces on the bandwagon's sides*

Illus. 7-13. *The last of the eight clown faces*

Illus. 7-14. *Close-up of one of the elephant heads on the sides of the bandwagon*

Illus. 7-15. *The other elephant head*

Illus. 7-16. *Bandwagon Box*

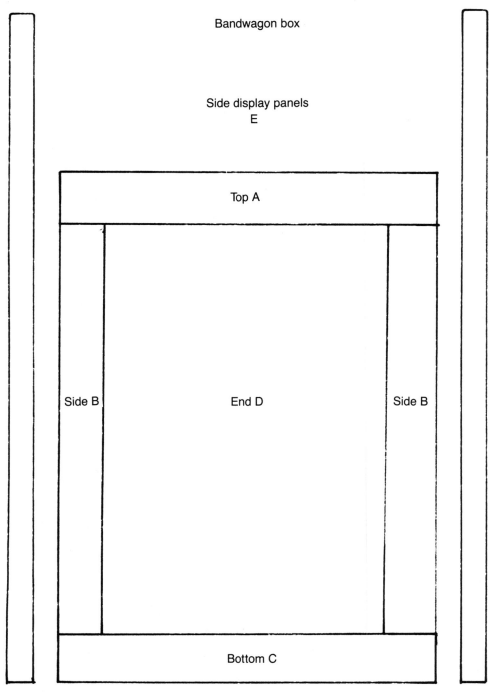

Bandwagon box

Side display panels
E

Top A

Side B   End D   Side B

Bottom C

End view
Full scale

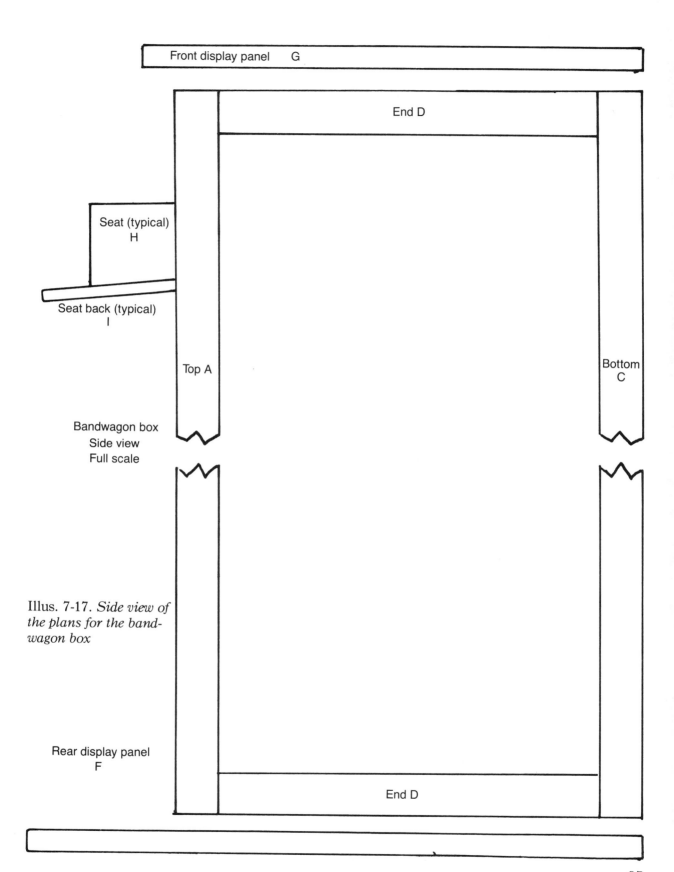

Front display panel   G

End D

Seat (typical)
H

Seat back (typical)
I

Top A

Bottom
C

Bandwagon box
Side view
Full scale

Illus. 7-17. *Side view of the plans for the band-wagon box*

Rear display panel
F

End D

Illus. 7-18. *Plans for
the bandwagon box*

	QUAN.	THICK.	WIDTH	LENGTH
A top	1	½″	4″	17½″
B sides	2	½″	4¼″	17½″
C bottom	1	½″	4″	17½″
D ends	2	½″	3″	4¼″
E side display panel	2	¼″	7″	18″
F rear display panel	1	¼″	4″	7″
G front display panel	1	¼″	4″	6″
H seats	5	1″	1″	4″
I seat backs	5	⅛″	2″	4″

Notes on building the box. Slant the back sides of the seats slightly as shown. Round the top ends of the seat backs for better appearance. Don't fasten the top of the box to the sides and ends. Leaving them unfastened will allow you to lift the entire seats section and band out for convenience in building, repairing, and/or shipping. The top will remain tightly in place, but you may want to secure it with at least one small screw for when you transport the box as a single unit. Locate the ⅛″ dowels so that they will be covered by faces or carvings when the display panels are attached to the box.

	QUAN.	THICK.	WIDTH	LENGTH
A lower 5th wheel	1	¼″	2″	3½″
B upper 5th wheel	1	¼″	2″ diameter	
C dowel	1	¼″	¼″	½″
D spring beam	2	¼″	¼″	3″
E springs	2	¼″	¼″	2½″
F dowel	1	⅛″	⅛″	½″
G tongue connector	1	½″	½″	1¼″
H tongue	1	¼″ dowel		14″
I axle	1	to fit wheel hub		
J axle	1	½″	½″	3″
K dowel	2	⅛″	⅛″	½″

Illus. 7-19. *Front-axle assembly*

Notes on front-axle and spring assembly. See Illustrations 7-20, 7-21, and 7-22 for details. The tongue connector (G) is sanded and drilled to fit. The top hole shown in Illus. 7-21 will receive the dowel that holds your evener in place. Don't cut the tongue (H) to length until your horses are in place. Sand the axle (J) and spring beam (D) to the configurations shown. You may want to use small dowels (K) to re-enforce all the glued connections. The dowels will give the joints more strength.

Illus. 7-20. *Front-axle assembly and spring pattern. You can make all four of the springs required in one cut. Trace the springs (as shown) on a scrap piece of ¼"-thick wood and double-tape a second piece to it. Saw on the lines shown, sand, and glue in place.*

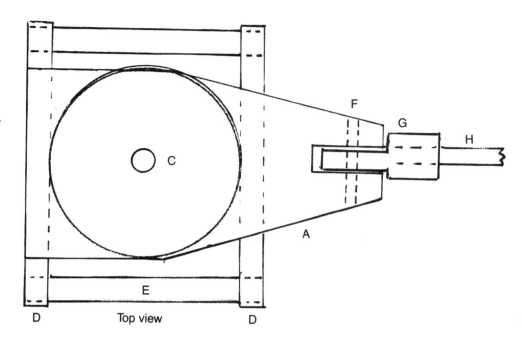

Top view

Illus. 7-21. *Side view of tongue connection*

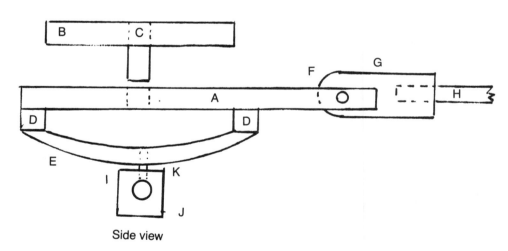

Side view

Illus. 7-22. *Rear-axle assembly*

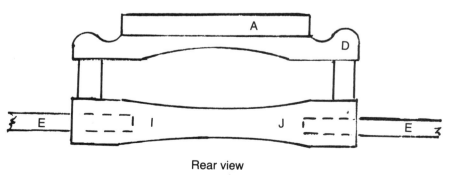

Rear view

	QUAN.	THICK.	WIDTH	LENGTH
A plate	1	¼″	2″	2½″
B *spring beams	2	¼″	¼″	3″
C *springs	2	¼″	¼″	2½″
D *dowel	1	⅛″	⅛″	½″
E *axle	1	to fit wheel hub		
F *axle	1	½″	½″	3″
G brake shoe	2	½″	½″	1½″
H brake hanger	2	½″	½″	**2″
I brake-wheel shaft	1	⅛″ dowel		**2½″
J brake wheel	1	⅛″	1″ diameter	

*same as front-axle assembly
**adjust length to fit

Notes on rear-axle assembly. Illus. 7-24 shows brake details. The brake wheel goes in the front left-hand corner of the top of the wagon's box. Adjust the length to fit your brakeman. As with the front axle, you may want to dowel the glued connections.

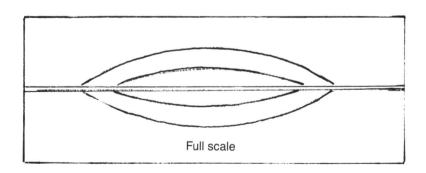

Full scale

Illus. 7-23. *Spring pattern (¼″ thick)*

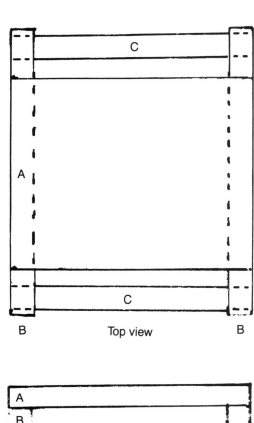

C

A

C

B   Top view   B

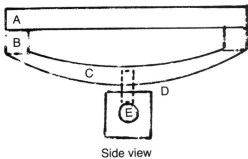

A

B

C

D

E

Side view

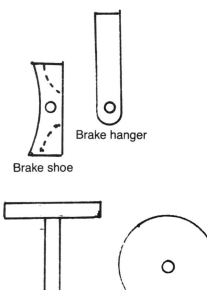

Brake hanger

Brake shoe

Brake wheel

Illus. 7-24. *Details of the rear-axle assembly and the brake*

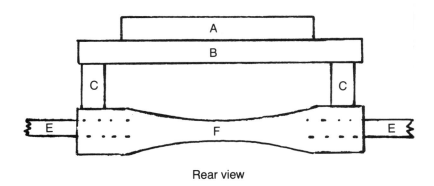

A

B

C   C

E   F   E

Rear view

Making Wooden Spoke Wheels

Good spoke wheels are difficult to find in stores or in catalogs. I was forced to make my own wheels because the ones I have found are either plastic or the wrong diameter. There are model rubber-tire wheels available, but I didn't want a rubber-tire wagon behind an eight-horse hitch. Illustrations 7-25 and 7-26 show the steps that I used to make the 2″ and 2½″ wheels I needed for this wagon. You may have your own wheel-making method, or you may even be able to find wheels to buy, but these wheels will work, and I think they give the wagon an "old" look that I wanted it to have. You'll find close-up finished wheels in Illustrations 7-27 and 7-28. Illus. 7-31 shows the rims being cut on the band saw.

Step 1: Double-tape two pieces of clear basswood ½″ × 3¼″ × 3¼″. Draw in the lines as shown (2½″, 2″, and a 1½″ circles) and dissect the circle for the number of spokes you want. The drawing is for an eight-spoke wheel. Saw out the 2½″ circle, staying outside the line.

Step 2: Sand the outside surfaces and extend the spoke lines across the face of the wheels. "X" the center of each rim on these lines.

Step 3: Use a bit that's slightly larger than the diameter of the spokes you're going to use (for a good loose fit) and drill each hole as shown. Be sure to go deep enough to go through both rims.

Step 4: Saw on the dotted line shown; be sure you start between two spoke holes.

Step 5: Remove the two rims and glue the sawed area back together. You now have two wooden rims with the spoke holes drilled in place.

Step 6: Use a ⅝″ dowel to make the hubs. Drill spoke holes to match the ones in the rims, using the dimensions shown. I made ten spoke wheels for my wagon, so I just sawed a shallow groove to receive the spokes. After the spokes were glued in place I used wood filler to fill the voids. This procedure is easier than locating and drilling the holes in the right place.

Step 7: Saw the dowel in 1″ lengths, drill the axle hole through the center, and taper the outside end on your disc sander, as shown.

Step 8: Assemble the wheel and hub dry and adjust the fit until the hub is centered. Now slide out one spoke at a time just enough to apply glue and then push it back in place. Glue the remaining spokes in the same way. You'll be very discouraged as you start assembling the wheel. The process is very sloppy, and you'll think that you're never going to get it all in place; but as you get more and more spokes in place, the wheel will become solid and strong. Adjusting the hub to the center can be difficult, but if the spokes fit loosely in the rim holes, it can be done. Make the 2″-diameter wheel the same way.

I've made many wheels using this method, and I've always painted the steel rims with black paint. For these wheels I used 36-gauge aluminum tooling foil. The roll of foil is 12″ wide and 36″ long, and it can easily be cut with scissors. Just cut ½″ strips and glue them on to make the steel rims. Aluminum tape would work well for this too; there's a thin aluminum-covered tape and a heavier, thicker aluminum tape. Both kinds come in rolls that are ¾″ wide.

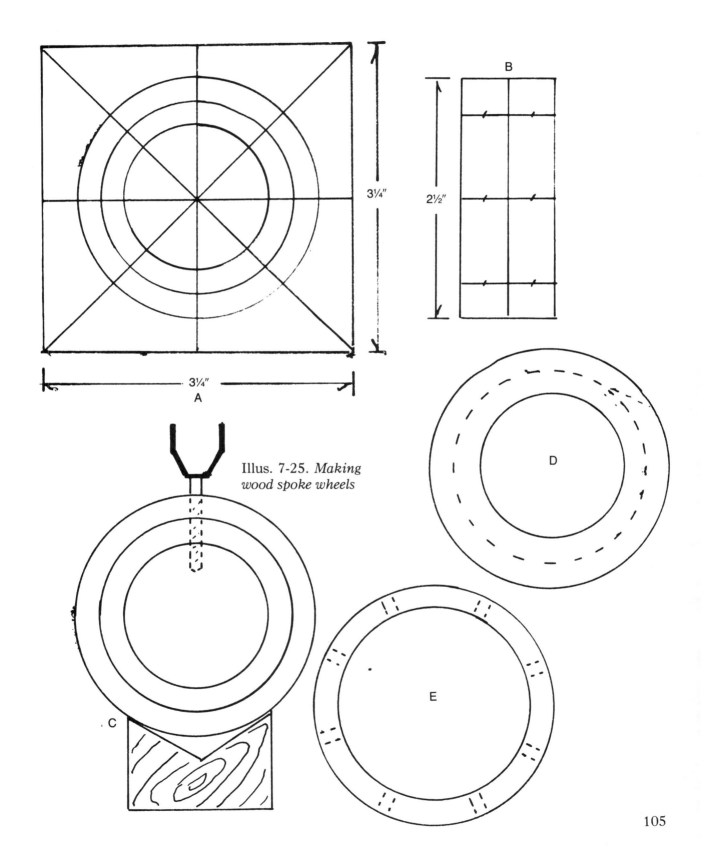

3¼"

2½"

3¼"

A

B

Illus. 7-25. *Making wood spoke wheels*

C

D

E

Illus. 7-26. *More details of the rear-wheel construction*

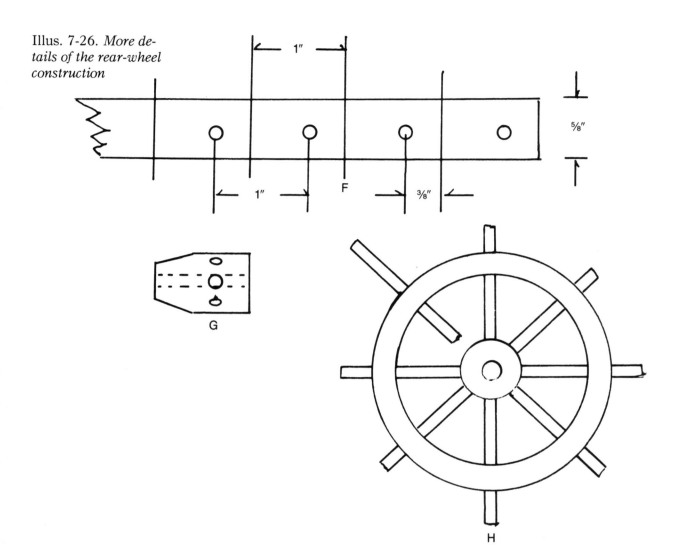

1"

1"

F

3/8"

5/8"

G

H

Illus. 7-27. *A close-up view of the front axle*

Illus. 7-28. *A close-up view of the tongue connector*

Illus. 7-29. *Top view of the tongue connector*

Illus. 7-30. *Detail of the rear wheel*

Illus. 7-31. *Making the wood-spoke wheels*

8
Displaying the Clowns

Whether you make your clowns for yourself, your friends, or for profit, you'll have to decide how you're going to display them. The simplest and probably the most common way to display them is to make an attractive base to support one (or a few) clowns. Illus. 8-1 shows the cop and the tramp mounted on a simple flat base. There are so many possibilities for different bases that I won't attempt to show them.

Illus. 8-1. *The cop chasing the tramp*

You'll be limited in your choice of bases only by your imagination.

Illustrations 8-2 and 8-3 show the way I have my clowns displayed now. I leave them unglued so that I can move them around just in case I ever want to. My circus parade is 5'10" long. The base is ¾" plywood boards 12" wide and cut in three pieces. The three sections split between the wagon and horses and between the back of the wagon and the trailer section. I have two dowels (similar to table-leaf pins) extending from the front and back sections that slide into holes in the center section. You can see the front section's dowels in Illus. 8-4. I put a ¼" oak border on the exposed plywood and I've made two wooden boxes that carry the entire parade if I want to move it. The parade has 23 clowns (including eight band members), a driver and a brakeman, and nine horses. The bandwagon has four elephants and eight clown faces.

Illus. 8-2. One side view of the bandwagon and the parade

Illus. 8-3. The other side of the bandwagon and the parade

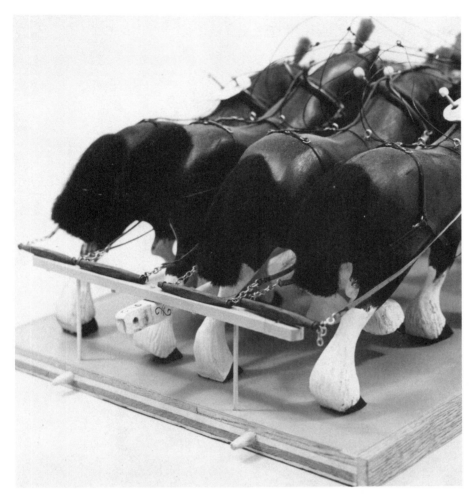

Illus. 8-4. *Rear view of the hitch that connects the draft horses to the section with the bandwagon*

Illus. 8-5 shows a demonstration of ten of the clowns used in the parade. The base contains a 1-rpm motor purchased at a model railroad store. The motor drives a plastic revolving cake tray (available almost anywhere). The tray turns very slowly, allowing views of the clowns from all angles.

You'll notice the eight-horse hitch (Illus. 8-7) and the performing circus horse in the several photos of the parade. The patterns and instructions for making these horses are contained in my last book, *Carving Horses and Carriages with Power Tools,* published by Sterling Publishing Co., Inc.

If you don't want to carve your own horses, you can buy very nice plastic draft horses in most toy stores, and they are the proper scale. My earlier book (mentioned above) has instructions for making the harnesses.

I would certainly like to see your ideas for displaying the clowns you make. Have fun making them—it's a circus!!

Illus. 8-5. *A selection of clowns displayed on a converted record player*

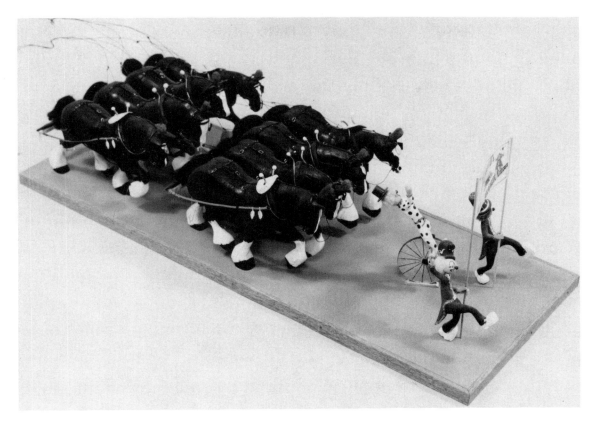

Illus. 8-6. *Front view of the eight-horse hitch*

Building the Calliope

Double-tape two pieces of ⅛"-thick wood 6″ × 4″. Trace and saw the sides as shown. While still taped together, drill the two ⅛" dowel holes for "G" dowels and the 1½" speaker hole shown.

I bought a small remote speaker that would fit in an area 3½″ × 2″ × 1¼". If you put a speaker in your calliope, be sure that it's this size before making the box. You may have to change the dimensions to fit your speaker. Cut the "B", "C" and "D" parts and drill a hole in the bottom for the speaker's plug to fit through (¾" on mine) and glue these parts together with the speaker installed. Glue the sides to this box and glue the "G" ⅛" dowels in place.

Glue the axle (E) and support stand dowel (F) in place as shown.

I used 2½" cast-aluminum wheels that are available in most catalogs and craft shops. Paint them red and simply nail them in place.

I painted my calliope silver and then decorated the sides with glitter three-dimensional paints. Craft shops have this and other brands of glitter paint that you just squeeze on the wood right from the tube. I used red to outline the sides, green to outline the speaker hole, and some gold for accent. This type paint is more commonly used for shirt decoration, but it works very well on wood.

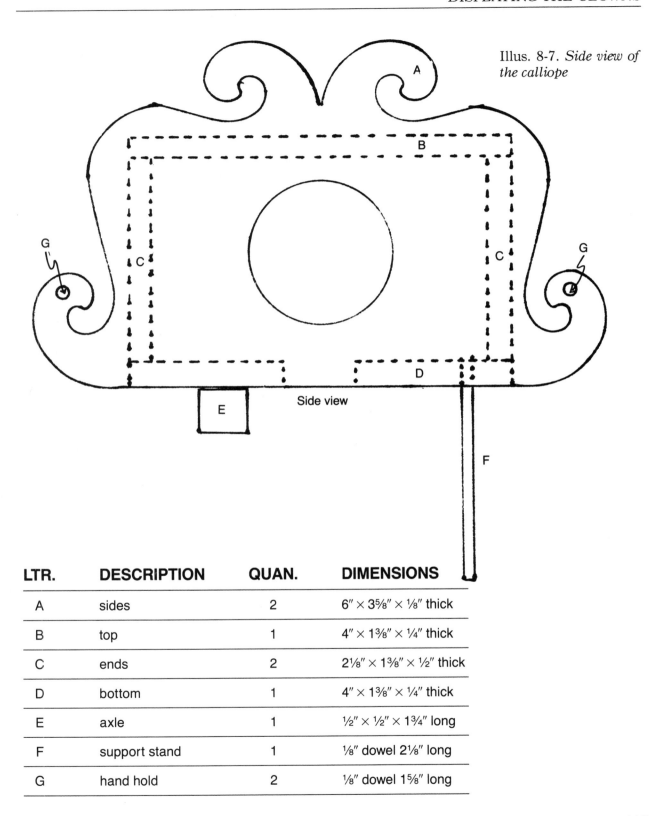

Illus. 8-7. *Side view of the calliope*

Side view

LTR.	DESCRIPTION	QUAN.	DIMENSIONS
A	sides	2	6″ × 3⅝″ × ⅛″ thick
B	top	1	4″ × 1⅜″ × ¼″ thick
C	ends	2	2⅛″ × 1⅜″ × ½″ thick
D	bottom	1	4″ × 1⅜″ × ¼″ thick
E	axle	1	½″ × ½″ × 1¾″ long
F	support stand	1	⅛″ dowel 2⅛″ long
G	hand hold	2	⅛″ dowel 1⅝″ long

117

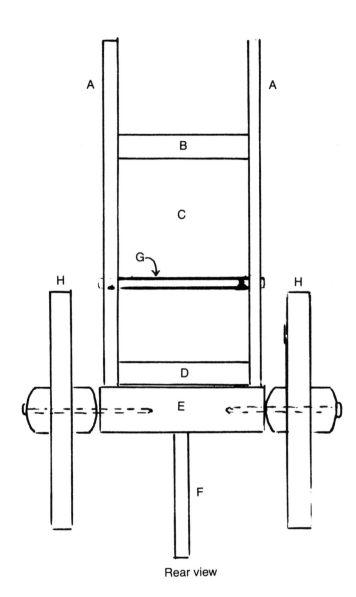

Illus. 8-8. *End view of the calliope*

Rear view

Horses

If you plan to carve your own horses you will find two profile patterns on pages 120 and 121. For the most effect, vary the leg positions and cut off and reglue the head positions.

Nearly any toy store sells plastic horses, including a Clydesdale trotting draft horse that would work very well in your parade. Your dealer may have to order the horses. Regardless of which type horse you use, you'll need to harness and hitch it to your bandwagon.

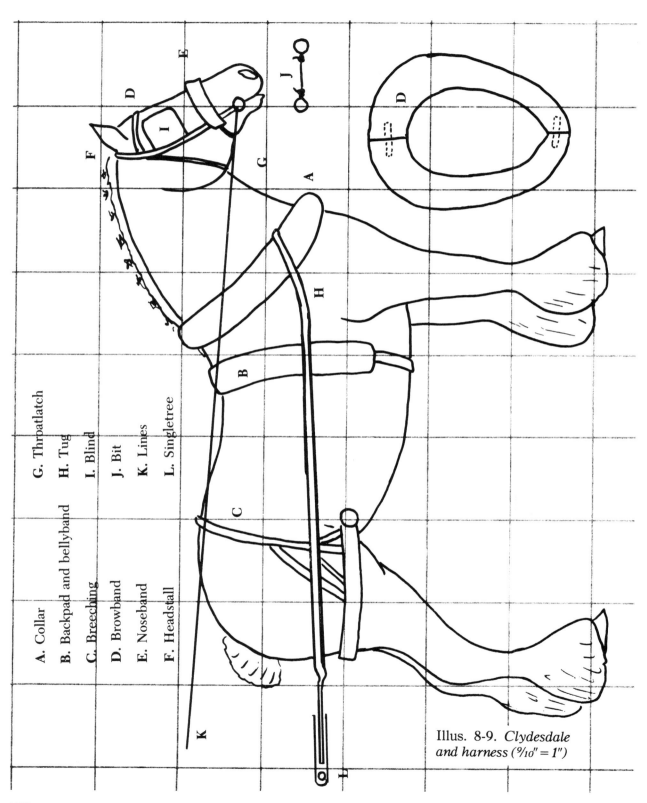

A. Collar
B. Backpad and bellyband
C. Breeching
D. Browband
E. Noseband
F. Headstall

G. Throatlatch
H. Tug
I. Blind
J. Bit
K. Lines
L. Singletree

Illus. 8-9. *Clydesdale and harness (⁹⁄₁₀″ = 1″)*

Illus. 8-10. *Trotting Clydesdale (full-size)*

Metric Equivalents

INCHES TO MILLIMETRES AND CENTIMETRES

MM—millimetres   CM—centimetres

Inches	MM	CM	Inches	CM	Inches	CM
⅛	3	0.3	9	22.9	30	76.2
¼	6	0.6	10	25.4	31	78.7
⅜	10	1.0	11	27.9	32	81.3
½	13	1.3	12	30.5	33	83.8
⅝	16	1.6	13	33.0	34	86.4
¾	19	1.9	14	35.6	35	88.9
⅞	22	2.2	15	38.1	36	91.4
1	25	2.5	16	40.6	37	94.0
1¼	32	3.2	17	43.2	38	96.5
1½	38	3.8	18	45.7	39	99.1
1¾	44	4.4	19	48.3	40	101.6
2	51	5.1	20	50.8	41	104.1
2½	64	6.4	21	53.3	42	106.7
3	76	7.6	22	55.9	43	109.2
3½	89	8.9	23	58.4	44	111.8
4	102	10.2	24	61.0	45	114.3
4½	114	11.4	25	63.5	46	116.8
5	127	12.7	26	66.0	47	119.4
6	152	15.2	27	68.6	48	121.9
7	178	17.8	28	71.1	49	124.5
8	203	20.3	29	73.7	50	127.0

Index

About the Author

Billy J. Smith was born and raised in northeast Iowa. Married to his wife, Doris, in 1948, they and their three children lived in Illinois, Wisconsin, and Nebraska before returning to Iowa to enter their own retail business. Smith sold his business in 1980 after spending 36 years as an agricultural equipment and storage salesman and sales manager. Smith and his wife now live in Arkansas, where they plan to spend their leisure time golfing, boating, and, of course, woodworking.

During his years in business, Smith wrote several sales-training manuals and held sales-training seminars nationwide. He became a popular banquet speaker and has spoken at county, state, and national agricultural meetings and conventions. Without formal art or drafting education, he became adept at designing, drawing, and selling automated animal feedlots and facilities.

After his retirement, he became interested in woodworking and, eventually, in wood-carving. Thanks to his experience in drawing and design, he was able to make his own patterns and he trained himself to carve with power tools. A lifetime of horse interest and ownership gave him a special insight to horse- and horse-related carving. He wrote *Carving Horses and Carriages with Power Tools* (Sterling Publishing Co., Inc.), wrote and published plans for a working miniature carousel, and published 24 folk-art wood-carving patterns. His carousel and carving patterns are advertised and sold through his own mail-order business.